Britannica Discovery Library

The Words Book

THIS WAY TO WORDS

1979 Printing
©1974 by Encyclopædia Britannica, Inc.
Copyright under International Copyright Union.
All rights reserved under Pan American and
Universal Copyright Conventions
by Encyclopædia Britannica, Inc.

International Standard Book Number: 0-85229-298-8
Printed in U.S.A.

Words

Hey, let's play baseball!

No, wait!
I want to go
to the circus!

Words are for talking —
for saying what you're thinking
or how you're feeling,
for asking questions,
and for answering them too.

3

Without words
how would you
talk with a friend?

Or tell about
a trip you took?

Without words how
would you describe
a red bike you want?

Or ask for the flavor
of ice cream cone
you like best?
(You would have
to point to it!)

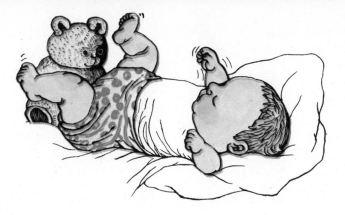

When you were a baby,
you couldn't talk.

You cried to let your mother know
that you were hungry. And reached
or pointed when you wanted something.

Now you can talk, but how did you learn?

5

You learned to talk by hearing your mother
and father say words over and over again.

You tried to make the sounds you heard.
And finally you did!

For a baby, learning
to talk is a little
like learning to walk.

A baby tries over and over
and over . . . and finally
learns to say a word
and to take a step.

Do you remember
when *you* couldn't
walk or talk?

Name-words

"Hey, you!"
"Who, me?" all four boys yelled.
"The boy at the top of the slide."
"Oh, my name is Bill."

Names are words that help to tell
people apart — to tell who's who.

Though people change the way they look,
their names usually stay the same.

With long or short hair,
Mary is still Mary,

Uncle Peter looks
different with a beard,
but his name is still Peter.

And even though you
change as you grow,
your name is still . . . .
What is it?

Things have names too.
And like the names of people, the names
of things help to tell them apart.

Do you know the names of all the things on these two pages?

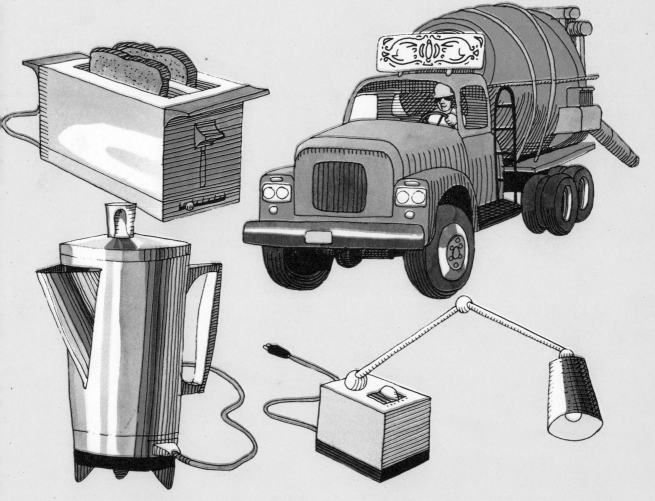

Action-words

Name-words tell people and things apart.
Action-words say what people and things are doing.

The king *eats* dinner.

Eats is an action-word.
It tells what the king
is doing.

Can you find all
the action-words
that follow?

The man *cooks* lunch.

The cat *purrs*.

The tailor *sews*.

The bird *watches* him.

The hammer *bangs*.

The men *work* hard.

What action-words tell
what each of the people
or animals on these pages
is doing?

What action-word tells
what *you* are doing now?

14

What-things-are-like Words

If two people are named Bill,
how can you tell them apart?
By the way they look, of course!

You might call one "Big Bill" and
the other "Little Bill." Or you
might say "Fat Bill" and "Skinny Bill."

big
little
fat
skinny

These are what-things-are-like words.

They tell how people and things look
and what they are like.

Find the
what-things-are-like
words below.

The *tall* man and the
short man are friends.

The *thirsty* man
drinks water.

The *red-haired* man
has freckles!

What-things-are-like words help to make
clear what you want to say.

If you told a friend
you saw a man with
a box, the friend
might imagine
this picture.

But if you used
what-things-are-like
words, your friend
might imagine this:
a *tired, bearded, old*
man carrying a *blue
polka-dot* box.

There are lots and lots of what-things-are-like words.

Here are some:

green	*young*
pretty	*funny*
striped	*happy*

Can you think of more?

Use some what-things-are-like words
to talk about these people and things.

Opposite-words

SOFT means fur and velvet too,
Butterfly wings and grass that's new,
Mushroom caps and clouds and custard,
Flower blooms and squishy mustard.

Now let's think of opposite things
Like stones and rocks and airplane wings,
Bricks and boards and hammers and nails,
Baseball bats and shiny pails.

HARD's the word that fits them all;
Hard is to soft as short is to tall—

OPPOSITE.

There are many
opposite-words like
young and *old*
or *early* and *late*.

Do you know the
opposite-words for:

      cold
      good
      sad
      fast
      before

Are there more opposite-words?

Where-things-are Words

This man is sitting
on a chair.
He's writing *on* paper.

The bear is riding *on* a bike. The umbrella is *over* the bear's head. And the bear's head is *under* the hat.

On, *over*, and *under* are where-things-are words. They tell exactly where things are!

Find the where-things-are words that follow.

The boat is *on* the river.
There are two people *in* the boat.

The boy is running *under* people's arms.
The people's arms are *over* the boy's head.

23

Peanuts grow UNDER the ground.

The spaceship is flying OVER the Earth.

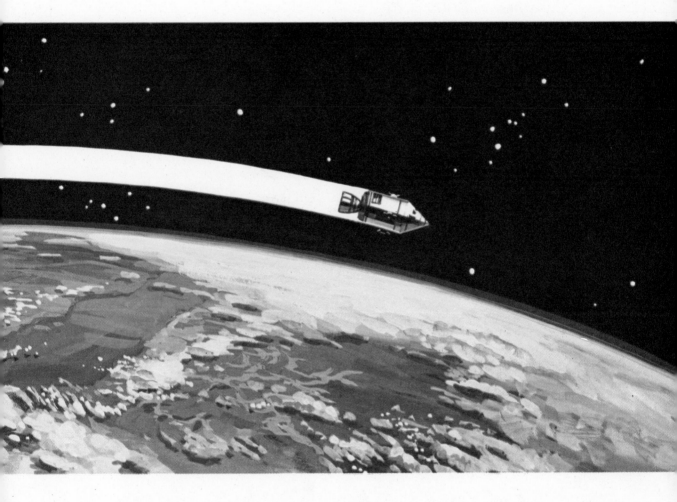

The girl *in* bed is *inside* the house.

The girl *at* the door is *outside* the house.

The boy has a cricket
inside a cage.

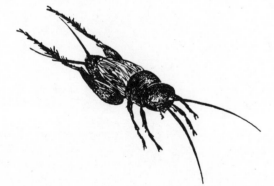

These crickets are *not*
inside a cage.
They are *outside* a cage.

27

ON
IN
AT
OVER
UNDER
INSIDE
OUTSIDE

Can you find people
in all these places
in this picture?

The Alphabet

Words are made from the letters of the alphabet.

The alphabet starts with the letter A. Do you know a word starting with an *a*?

How about: *a*nt, *a*irplane, *a*lligator

An *a* can come in the middle or at the end of a word too—as in c*a*ke or sof*a*.

After A comes B. Find every *b* in these words:

boy, baby, bubble rubber, bathtub

Next come C and D,
Then E, F, and G.
Can you find these letters
in the words you see?

Carol chose chocolate
cake and crunchy candy.

David and Dottie
danced day and night.

Elephants eat every
scrambled egg they see!

Fred was furious. So
he fought with a friend.

Grapes grow on
gorgeous green vines.

Then H and I,
J, K, and L.
You know them already?
Oh my, that's swell!

Harriet helped Harry with
his handshake. Hurray!

I like Ida's eyes.
Ivan itches if he sits
in poison ivy!

Jack just jumped over a
pile of juicy jellybeans.

Kevin knows that Katie
bakes cakes and cookies.

Larry loves Laura Lee.
How lovely!

M and N,
O, P, and Q
Come next in the whole
Alphabet for you.

Micky climbed over a
mountain for some
milk and muffins.

Never knit a necktie
for a snake. It has
no neck!

Oranges or doughnuts
are so good to eat.

Pancakes with plums are
scrumptious for parties.

Quiet ducks quack when
the earth quakes.

R and S,
T, U, and V
Are the next letters
As you can see.

Rose wants red ribbons
for her birthday.

Snakes hiss sometimes,
and seals swim fast.

Tom telephoned Teresa.
They talked about trains.

Usually you can
outrun a unicorn!

Vicky loves velvety
violets very much.

W and X,
Y and Z are last.
Practice your letters—
You'll learn them fast.

What *would* Walter *want*
with a *wet w*affle?
*W*ho kno*w*s!

*X*avier and Ma*x* arrived
in a ta*x*i e*x*actly on
time. E*x*cellent!

*Y*ou ma*y y*earn to eat
*y*umm*y y*ellow egg *y*olks.

Di*zz*y *z*ebras *z*ig*z*ag
in *z*oos.

Putting Words Together

Putting letters together makes words like

c-a-t or

And putting words together so that
they mean something makes a sentence.

Cat have a I is not a sentence.
It's just a silly-sounding group of words.
But *I have a cat* is a sentence.
The words mean something.

Can you make up another sentence with
the word *cat*? How about another sentence
with the words *brown* and *dog*?

cat

Below you'll find
some jumbled-up words
that sound funny.
Can you make them
sound like sentences?

The dog named is Freddy

A hill on the man stands

A window looks out of a man

Under the sign two are people

Here are some words in the right order.
But to make sentences, you need to add
some more words. Can you do it?

The ＿＿ is shining.

＿＿ package has a pink ＿＿.

The girl ＿ running ＿＿ the field.

＿＿ boy ＿＿ his brother cross the ＿＿.

Putting Sentences Together

Putting words together can make sentences.
And putting sentences together can make
lots of things—

a letter to your friend,

Toronto, Ontario
January 16, 1975

Dear Johnny,
  I bet you are
glad to hear from
me. How do you
like California?
Is it warm there?
It's snowing here.

or a song that you like,

Row, row, row your boat,
Gently down the stream—

a riddle like this one:

What's the difference between
an elephant and a flea?
Elephants can have fleas, but
fleas can't have elephants!

or a funny poem:

There was an old man with a beard,
Who said, "It is just as I feared!
Two owls and a hen, four larks and a wren
Have all built their nests in my beard."

Putting sentences together can also make stories that are fun to hear or to tell.

Here's one story that you might like.

Stone Soup

A tired traveler trudged
over hills and through forests
all day, hoping to find food
and a place to rest. It grew
dark, and he had almost given
up hope when, suddenly, he
saw a tiny cottage.

"How good it will be,"
he thought, "to warm myself
in front of a fire and to have
a good meal."

But when he knocked at
the door, the old woman who
lived in the cottage cried,
"Go away! I don't like
strangers here."

"I'm cold and tired and half-starved," said the traveler. "Won't you let me in and give me a bit of bread?"

"I'm a poor woman and haven't any food even for myself. You must go somewhere else," said the old woman.

"But I've walked so far already. May I at least rest here for a while and warm myself?" begged the traveler.

"Oh, very well," grumbled the woman, "come in, but don't ask for food again because I have none."

Once inside the cottage, the traveler could see that the woman was not so poor as she pretended. He settled himself before the fireplace and said, "Since you have shared your fire with me, I will share a secret with you. Lend me a pot and a spoon."

The woman grumbled, but soon brought a pot and a spoon. The traveler filled the pot with water and hung it over the fire. Then he reached into his pocket and pulled out a small stone. He dropped the stone into the water and began stirring the pot with the spoon.

"What is that supposed to be?" demanded the woman.

"Stone soup," replied the traveler.

"Stone soup? I never heard of such a thing! It doesn't look fit to eat," said the woman.

"Oh, stone soup is wonderful," said the traveler. "And stones like this one make the very best soup. I've used this stone for several days so the soup may be a bit thin. But even so, it will be a treat."

He continued to stir the pot and after a few minutes said, "It's coming along nicely. Too bad we don't have a little barley to thicken it with. But, of course, there's no sense in wishing."

"Come to think of it, I may have a *little* barley," said the woman. She left the room and soon returned with a cup full of barley.

"That's wonderful!" said the traveler, adding the barley to the water. He stirred a few minutes more and then said, "Yes, indeed, this is fine! It's just too bad we don't have a turnip and a potato or two. They make ordinary stone soup into a feast, but this will do."

"Well," said the woman, "maybe I overlooked something." Again she left the room, and when she returned, she gave the traveler two turnips, three potatoes, and a carrot.

"Oh my, what soup we shall have!" he cried, putting the vegetables into the pot. The woman grew hungrier by the minute, watching the traveler stir the soup.

"I was just thinking how nice it would be," said the traveler, "to have a piece of meat in the soup. But, then, we mustn't worry over what we don't have."

"Just a moment," said the woman. She dashed out and back in again with several large chunks of meat.

"Glorious!" exclaimed the traveler, "This stone soup will be fit for the Queen!" He continued to stir the pot and at last announced the soup was ready.

They sat down to their meal and ate and ate. And when they had finished all the soup, the woman said, "That was the most delicious soup I have ever tasted. And to think that it was made with just a stone!"

"It's easy," said the traveler, smiling to himself, "so long as you use the right sort of stone. . . *and* have a little something to flavor it with!"

Books

Putting sentences together can also make up
what you're holding in your hand—a whole book.

A *library* is a place where there
are lots and lots of books—
so many books that you may need help
in finding the one you want to read.

In a library there's always a man or woman called a *librarian* who can help you find the book you want.

Tell the librarian the name of the book you want to read.

THE DINOSAUR'S DUCK

The librarian will
show you where it
is on the shelves—

THE DINOSAUR'S DUCK

then help you write your
name on the card you'll
find inside the book.

And you can borrow the book to read at home.

Words That Sound Alike

Cats wear hats
and rats wear spats.

Cats, *hats*, *rats*, and *spats* are
words that sound alike. They *rhyme*.

Lots of words rhyme:

    word — bird
    song — long
    mug — rug
    silly — Billy

What word could finish this rhyme?

Something I'd like
Is a shiny new _____.

Can you finish
this rhyme?

I float in the sky
Like a pretty round moon.
Can you guess what I am?
I'm a bright red _____.

How about this one?

I once saw a bird
Flying ever so high.
It flew and flew
All over the _____.

Here are some funny
rhymes called *limericks*.

Thin little Billy Muldoon
Was carried away by a b'loon.
　"Good-bye, Billy dear,"
　Said his mom, with a tear,
"Please write when you get to the moon."

There was an old man of Peru
Who dreamed he was kissing his shoe.
　He awoke in the night
　In a terrible fright,
And found it was perfectly true!

There was young lady of Crete
Who was exceedingly neat.
　When she got out of bed,
　She stood on her head
To make sure of not soiling her feet.

Some limericks are very
hard to say. They're
called *tongue twisters.*

A tutor who tooted the flute
Tried to tutor two tooters to toot.
  Said the two to the tutor,
  "Is it harder to toot or
To tutor two tooters to toot?"

Here are some more tongue twisters
that don't rhyme. Can you say them?

A big, black bug bit a big, black bear.

Two terribly talkative tigers
talked till time for tea.

She sells seashells by the seashore.

How much wood would a woodchuck
chuck if a woodchuck could chuck
wood?

Do you know any more tongue twisters?

A D-elightful Story

Detective Dan Dover went door to door looking for the famous "Dudley Diamond" and discovered:

a dancer. . .

a dwarf with a dagger. . .

a deep-sea diver. . .

a drummer. . .

and a damsel in distress.

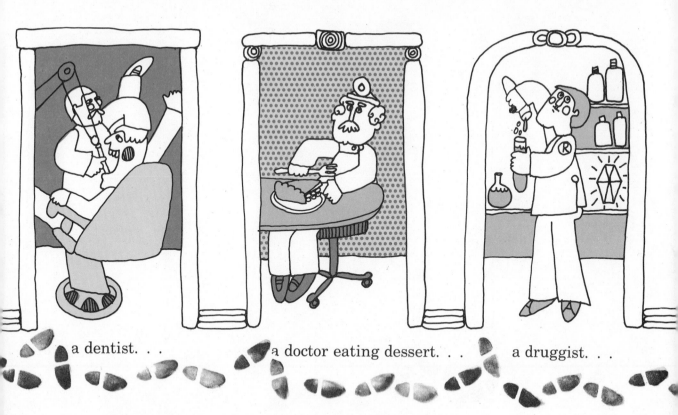

a dentist. . .   a doctor eating dessert. . .   a druggist. . .

Finally he discovered the diamond lying in the dirt near
the railroad tracks. Go back and look through each doorway carefully.
See if you can guess who put the diamond where Detective Dover found it.
And see how many "d" words you can find in this story.

So many things to do with words!
You've only just begun.